HISTORY IN ART

ANCIENT GREECE

D0486797

Raintree

ANDREW LANGLEY

ALIS

1617596

www.raintreepublishers.co.uk
Visit our website to find out more information about Raintree books.

To order:
☎ Phone 44 (0) 1865 888112
▤ Send a fax to 44 (0) 1865 314091
🖳 Visit the Raintree Bookshop at www.raintreepublishers.co.uk to browse our catalogue and order online.

Produced for Raintree by
White-Thomson Publishing Ltd
Bridgewater Business Centre, 210 High Street,
Lewes, East Sussex, BN7 2NH.

First published in Great Britain by Raintree part
of Harcourt Education.
Raintree is a registered trademark of Harcourt Education Ltd.

© Harcourt Education Ltd 2005
First published in paperback in 2006
The moral right of the proprietor has been asserted.

All rights reserved. No part of this publication may be reproduced, stored in a retrieval system, or transmitted in any form or by any means, electronic, mechanical, photocopying, recording, or otherwise, without either the prior written permission of the publishers or a licence permitting restricted copying in the United Kingdom issued by the Copyright Licensing Agency Ltd, 90 Tottenham Court Road, London W1T 4LP (www.cla.co.uk).

Editorial: Catherine Burch and Diyan Leake
Consultant: Dr Philip de Souza, Lecturer in Classics, University College Dublin
Design: Michelle Lisseter and Richard Parker
Page make-up: Mind's Eye Design Ltd, Lewes
Picture Research: Elaine Fuoco-Lang
Map artwork: Martin Darlison, Encompass Graphics
Production: Amanda Meaden
Originated by Dot Gradations
Printed and bound in China
by South China Printing Company

ISBN 1 844 43359 5 (hardback)
09 08 07 06 05
10 9 8 7 6 5 4 3 2 1

ISBN 1 844 43364 1 (paperback)
09 08 07 06
10 9 8 7 6 5 4 3 2 1

British Library Cataloguing in Publication Data
Langley, Andrew
History in Art: Ancient Greece
1 844 433595
A full catalogue record for this book is available from the British Library.

Langley, Andrew

Ancient Greece /
Andrew Langley

J938

1617596

Acknowledgements
The publishers would like to thank the following for permission to reproduce photographs (t) = top (b) = bottom): AKG pp. **8**, **9** (Erich Lessing), **12** (Cameraphoto), **15**(b) (John Hios), **23**(t) (John Hios), **24**(t), **38**(t) (Erich Lessing); Ancient Art and Architecture pp. **10** (Brian Gibbs), **16** (B. Norman), **30**(t & b) (Ronald Sheridan); Bridgeman Art Library pp. **4**(t), **5**, **6**, **7**(b), **11**, **13**, **14**, **15**(t) (Lauros/Giraudon), **20** (Alinari), **21**(t) (Peter Willi), **21**(b), **22** (Peter Willi), **25**, **24**(b) (Giraudon), **25**(b) (Giraudon), **26**, **27** (Bonhams, London, UK), **28**, **29**(t), **29**(b) (Peter Willi), **31**, **32**, **33**(t & b), **34**, **35**(b) (Bildarchiv Steffens), **36** (Lauros/Giraudon), **37**(t), **37**(b) (Lauros/Giraudon), **38**(b) (Peter Willi), **39** (Bildarchiv Steffens), **40**, **41**, **42** (Alinari); Harcourt/Corbis **17**(t); Harcourt Education Ltd. **18**; Museum of Fine Arts, Houston, Texas, USA/www.bridgeman.co.uk pp. **43**; The Art Archive pp. **19** (Museo Nazionale Terme Rome/Dagli Orti), **23**(b) (Museo Nazionale Taranto/Dagli Orti), **35**(t) (National Archaeological Museum Athens/Dagli Orti); The Detroit Institute of Arts, USA/www.bridgeman.co.uk pp. **7**(t); WTPix pp. **4**(b), **17**(b).

Cover photograph of an ancient Greek death mask reproduced with permission of AKG.

Every effort has been made to contact copyright holders of any material reproduced in this book. Any omissions will be rectified in subsequent printings if notice is given to the publishers.

The publisher would like to thank Dr Christina Haywood, Curator of the Classical Museum, University College Dublin, for her assistance in the preparation of this book.

Disclaimer
All the Internet addresses (URLs) given in this book were valid at the time of going to press. However, due to the dynamic nature of the Internet, some addresses may have changed, or sites may have changed or ceased to exist since publication. While the author, the packager and publishers regret any inconvenience this may cause readers, no responsibility for any such changes can be accepted by either the author, the packager or the publishers.

The paper used to print this book comes from sustainable resources.

Contents

Words included in the glossary are in **bold** the first time they appear in each chapter.

Art as evidence

'Future generations will marvel at us,' predicted Pericles, leader of Athens in about 440 BC, 'as the present age marvels at us now.' The Greeks themselves knew they were something special. Indeed it is amazing that two thousand years after the decline of the Greek **civilization**, its powerful influence can still be seen in modern **politics** and ideas, art and architecture, sport and theatre.

How do we know about such an ancient civilization? What is left behind to tell us about this long-gone age? **Archaeologists** have found the ruins of many great buildings, and thousands of paintings, sculptures, pots and other remains of the ancient Greek world. The writings of Greek historians, statesmen, poets and playwrights survive, but the biggest and most varied record lies in the work of the artists, which is certainly some of the most outstanding ever created. Their marble statues, painted pottery and massive temples still inspire artists today, and provide superb source material about the history, **mythology** and daily life of ancient Greece.

Greek inspiration

Greek art is all around us. Throughout history, artists of all kinds have used the methods, subjects and inspiration of the ancient Greeks in their work. **Renaissance** sculptors such as Michelangelo were deeply influenced by Greek models. The head of Michelangelo's statue of David (right), completed in 1504, was inspired by the Greeks.

▼ The Acropolis ('stronghold on a hill'), topped by the Parthenon, dominates the skyline of modern Athens. It is one of the most famous historic sites in the world.

Steep rock sides of the Acropolis   Fortified walls at the top   The Erechtheion   The Parthenon

Pictures of the past

The pictures on vases and other pottery show in wonderful detail what the Greeks ate and wore, and how they entertained themselves, as well as countless episodes from the myths. Mythical adventures and important moments in Greek history are illustrated in carvings and wall paintings. We deduce (or work out) from the many nude male statues the Greeks' reverence for the human body. Great buildings, such as the Parthenon in Athens and the Theatre at Epidauros, tell us

a huge amount about Greek religion and public life. All the same, this treasury of source material must be treated with caution. It would be wrong solely to rely on **artefacts** like these to give us a complete and realistic picture of Greek life. Vivid though they are, the pictures and statues tell us only part of the story. Greek sculptors wanted to portray human beauty in their work, but this does not mean that all Greek youths were beautiful!

We have to interpret what we see, and look beyond the surface, because these works of art also give us less obvious information. By studying them we can find out how they were made, who made them and what materials were used. This provides us with evidence of what sort of technology was available to the Greeks – for **casting bronze** statues, turning clay vases, or transporting and lifting big blocks of marble.

The goddess Nike (Victory) carrying a garland

◀ The winged Nike, Greek symbol of victory in battle, is shown in flight in this delicate vase painting from about 430 BC.

Bronze tripod, with legs fixed to stone base

Stone column supports bowl for sacrificial offerings

Gold patterns at the top and bottom act as frames for the picture

Learning the secrets

The art treasures of ancient Greece come in many different shapes and sizes. There are vast temples and tiny carved gemstones, painted vases and marble statues. All of these things – if we look at them properly – give us not only a lot of pleasure but also vital clues about Greek life and manners. Before studying this rich source material, we have to decide how informative it may be by answering some questions.

Who made these artefacts? We know the names of some of the artists. A few vase painters put signatures on their work ('Exekias painted me', reads one vase), but most of the rest are unknown, and probably saw themselves as merely craft workers rather than artists.

There were, however, many sculptors such as Praxiteles, and wall painters such as Zeuxis, who were celebrities throughout Greece.

Who did these artists and craftsmen work for? Only the rich and powerful (including kings and queens) could afford to pay the best sculptors and painters. They bought the most beautifully painted vases and commissioned carved memorial stones for their family graves. By far the biggest employer was the state. Public money was used to pay for the building of enormous temples such as the Parthenon, the great temple in the city of Athens, and to fill them with magnificent statues and wall paintings.

▼ A wall painting showing a procession of warriors from a 4th century BC Greek tomb in Paestum, southern Italy.

Greaves to protect lower legs

Breastplate to protect upper body

Decorated shield made of bronze and wood

Long spear for thrusting and stabbing rather than throwing

Bronze helmet

Mounted warrior has no stirrups

Attendant carrying a torch

Ornate stopper to seal oil inside

Examining the evidence

Temples, sculptures and other objects can tell us about Greek history, mythology and daily life – as long as we know what to look for. This amphora, or two-handled storage jar, shows athletes running a race. It is one of many such jars that were produced to hold the olive oil made from the fruit of the sacred olive grove dedicated to the goddess Athena. The oil-filled jar was presented to winners of the athletic events at the Panathenaic Festival in Athens, held every four years in honour of Athena, the city's patron goddess.

Athletes normally wore no clothes while competing

The long stride and high arm action indicate that they are sprinting

Amphora was given as a prize to a victorious athlete

◀ A Panathenaic amphora showing athletes running. On the other side is a picture of Athena, goddess of the city of Athens. The style of the images, painted in black, reveals that the vase was probably made in about 550 BC.

How has Greek art survived?

In the 2000 years since the ancient Greek civilization faded, many works of art have disappeared. They have been smashed or stolen, or have simply crumbled away. The Parthenon suffered huge damage from a Venetian artillery shell in 1687. Yet a vast amount remains, and fresh finds continue to be made. Since the early 1800s, archaeologists have excavated ancient sites such as Delphi, Ephesus and Thebes, and rediscovered many masterpieces of pottery, sculpture and architecture lying hidden in the earth. Other treasures, such as a bronze statue of Zeus, have been found lying under the sea. This painting from the palace at Knossos shows an elaborate **ritual** involving a bull and leaping athletes. Nobody knows exactly what the ritual involved.

The story of ancient Greece

The country we now know as Greece is made up of the mainland and many islands, which are scattered throughout the Aegean and Adriatic Seas. Ancient Greece, however, was not a unified country nor, a centrally controlled empire like Rome.

Myceneans

The first great **civilization** on the mainland did not appear until about 1600 BC. An **immigrant** group of settlers established their power in the south of Greece and built several important towns. We call them the Mycenaeans, after their hilltop stronghold of Mycenae.

Almost nothing was known about these people until the late 19th century, when **archaeologists** began to excavate Mycenae and nearby sites. They found sensational things – royal tombs crammed with gold and other treasures, pottery, fortified walls (some as much as eight metres thick) and a massive palace. Most famous of all was the Lion Gate at the main entrance to the palace, with its huge **lintel** topped with a triangular **relief carving** of two lions.

▼ The Lion Gate was the magnificent entrance to the fortress of Mycenae. The city walls were so massive that in later years people thought they could only have been built by giants.

Two relief carvings of lionesses, now headless

The triangular gap around the carvings helps to spread the weight on the enormous lintel stone underneath

The huge stone blocks of the walls are cut to fit precisely together

The lintel, a piece of solid stone 4.5 m long and 2 m wide

Thin gold sheet hammered
to show features

◀ This gold death mask found at Mycenae was
once thought to show the face of Agamemnon,
the king who led the Greeks at Troy. In fact, it
is from a much earlier date than the Trojan
Wars can possibly have been.

Gold untarnished despite being
buried for thousands of years

Funeral mask
does not show
dead man's
true features

A close study of these magnificent
discoveries gives us a picture of a
wealthy, warlike and well-organized
society. There are gold masks, which
probably depict the faces of Mycenaean
kings and heroes, and emphasize their power
and authority. Pictures on silver ornaments and
vases show Mycenaean soldiers in action, well armed
with chariots, helmets, spears and shields. Delicately
carved ivory pieces which have come from the East
have been found, telling us that there must have been
trading contacts with lands such as Egypt and the
Levant (the eastern Mediterranean).

The Dark Ages and after

By about 1100 BC the power of the Mycenaeans had
gone. The palaces and fortresses were destroyed and
the villages abandoned, possibly after a savage civil war.
Greece moved into what historians have called the
Dark Ages, which lasted for more than three centuries.
Archaeologists know very little about this period.
Some Greeks moved overseas to escape the poverty
of their native land.

The Trojan War

The **epic** of the Greeks' siege of Troy is one of the best-
known stories in the world. It tells of a war lasting nine
years, with a cast of characters including Achilles,
Helen of Troy, Odysseus and Ajax, as well as gods and
goddesses. No one knows for certain if and when the
conflict actually took place. Archaeologists have found
evidence that a city on the site of Troy, on the coast of
Asia Minor (or modern Turkey), was destroyed in
about 1250 BC. Homer's poem *The Iliad* tells episodes
from the siege of Troy, but this was probably written at
least 400 years afterwards. Whatever the truth of the
Trojan Wars, their heroes, heroines and deeds became
a central part of Greek **mythology**, and the key scenes
appear in many sculptures and vase paintings.

The birth of the city-state

Greece is a land of steep mountain ranges, with relatively few areas of flat land that can be farmed between them. Most of the early communities grew up in these valleys, or on the narrow coastal plains, but the mountainous landscapes kept them separate from each other. So it was that these scattered communities developed into city-states with strong individual identities.

Polis

This kind of independent society, which controlled an area of country around a fortified centre, was called a *polis*. Some were very small in size, but each ran its own affairs, with its own army, parliament, laws and coinage. Many built their strongholds on a hill with steep sides and a flat top. This was called the *acropolis* or 'high city'.

▼ The ruins of the Temple of Apollo at Corinth, with the city's *acropolis* (the Acrocorinth) rising up behind. Corinth controlled the narrow strip of land joining the Peloponnese to the rest of Greece, which is why it became powerful during the 5th century BC.

The mountain of the Acrocorinth

Doric **columns** of Temple of Apollo, once the centre of the ancient city

Surrounded by a thick wall, the *acropolis* was an ideal spot for people to shelter when attacked by enemies. It was also a centre of worship, with the main temples and other important buildings grouped there. The cost, labour and care put into these structures show the central importance of religion in the city-states. Among the best known of these strongholds are the Acropolis in Athens, the Acrocorinth near the city of Corinth and Lindos on the island of Rhodes.

Power to the people

It is from *polis* that we get the modern word **politics** – the science of running a state or community. The Greeks developed this science, exploring the meaning of justice and law, and examining new and fairer ways of governing people. Kings and queens disappeared early in Greek history, and power came into the hands of the wealthy **aristocrats** (nobles). The poor had no political rights, owned no land, and were virtually slaves for their rich rulers.

▶ This vase has survived intact because it was placed in a grave.

The 'Key' motif was very popular in Greek art

Zones of different patterns cover the whole vase

From about 650 BC, the aristocrats found themselves being pushed aside by the 'tyrants' (from the Greek word *turannos*), who seized power by force. Many tyrants were actually popular at first. In Corinth, the tyrant threw out the aristocrats, who were hated by the people. In Megara and Samos, the new ruler installed a water supply. It was not long, however, before the tyrants lost the support of the people, and an early form of **democracy** (rule by the people) began to be introduced, with voting rights for all (wealthy) male citizens. Greece's greatest period was about to begin.

Inspiration from the East

As trade routes grew and overseas settlements were founded, pottery, jewellery and other fine things were **imported** into Greece, and the influence of other cultures begins to show in Greek art. Early sculptures of male nudes were closely modelled on statues from Egypt. Vase decorations in the 'Geometric' style (see jug, right, made in about 730 BC) with formal patterns and matchstick figures, gave way to more realistic and detailed pictures of humans and animals, inspired by work from Assyria. This developed into what is known as 'black-figure' painting, with the figures drawn in outlines of black paint.

Invasions and civil war

During the 5th century BC two wars transformed ancient Greece. At the centre of both were the two biggest and most powerful city-states – Athens and Sparta. By 500 BC Athens and Sparta were growing much faster than the other cities, but in very different ways. Athens, with its new democratic government, was becoming wealthy through overseas trade. Sparta was ruled by two kings, and used its permanent and highly trained army to subdue neighbouring states.

The Persian Wars

At this time Persia had built up a huge empire that stretched into Asia Minor, and included some of the Greek settlements. In 499 BC these cities rebelled against Persian rule and were given help by Athens. This angered Darius, the Persian emperor, and in 490 BC he sent his army to punish the Greeks. The Athenians defeated the invaders on the plain of Marathon, north of the city.

There was still enormous danger. For the first time in Greek history, over 30 cities throughout the land – notably Athens, Sparta and Corinth – agreed to join forces to fight the invader. In 480 BC Darius invaded again with an even bigger force. The Spartans held up the Persian advance with a heroic stand at Thermopylae, and then the combined Greek navy destroyed the enemy fleet at Salamis. The following year the Greek army (led by a Spartan) won a decisive victory at Plataia.

Curved stern ornament, or aplustre

Soldiers defending their ship with spears and stones

Sailors scrambling aboard the ship

▲ A stone relief panel, carved to decorate a tomb in the 2nd century BC. It illustrates a naval battle between the Greeks and their enemies.

The Peloponnesian Wars

The defeat of the Persians brought great prestige to Athens, which became the leading power in eastern Greece. This was the period when Athens erected magnificent new buildings such as the Parthenon. But as the city grew stronger and richer, her neighbours (especially Sparta) grew jealous and the long Peloponnesian War began.

The war lasted for 27 years. At first the Athenians refused to fight on land, relying on their strong navy. But then Athens mounted a disastrous expedition to conquer Sicily. The Athenian fleet became trapped inside the harbour at Syracuse and both fleet and army were wiped out. Athens was permanently weakened. By 404 BC the great city of Athens was forced to surrender.

Ancient Greece was never a united country. After crushing Athens, Sparta began to bully its allies and even quarrelled with the powerful Persians. The chaos continued for another 20 years, until out of the remote state of Macedonia arose a strong new leader.

King Philip II of Macedonia had a powerful army which subdued the states around him. But just at the height of his success, Philip was murdered. He was succeeded by his 20-year-old son, Alexander.

Athens' Golden Age

After the Persian Wars, Athens entered its 'Golden Age'. Under the leadership of Pericles, Athens was made an artistic show-place.

- The temples on the Acropolis, ruined by the Persian attacks, were replaced with a breathtaking group of buildings including the Parthenon and the Propylaia gateway, shown here. This was the grand entrance to the Acropolis, and it boasted five elaborate doorways, a blue ceiling covered with gold stars, and a picture gallery.
- Pheidias and other brilliant sculptors carved reliefs and statues, including a giant figure of Athena and Meyron's *Discus Thrower*.

▼ Major cities and important sites of the ancient Greek world.

Marching to India

Alexander the Great, as he came to be known, turned out to be one of the greatest military leaders in history. He first established complete command in Greece by putting down rebel states. Then he took 37,000 soldiers across the sea to conquer the Persians. One victory followed another, and by 332 BC Alexander had reached Egypt, where he founded a new city called Alexandria.

Alexander's conquests continued into the east. He marched his army up into the snowy mountains of Afghanistan, down again on to the plains of Pakistan and across the Indus River into India itself. Finally his exhausted troops rebelled, and in 324 BC he turned and headed for home. Alexander died the following year, aged only 32. He had created a massive empire, but there was no new leader strong enough to keep it together and soon the different regions were fighting each other.

▼ A detail from the Alexander Mosaic, showing the Persian King Darius under attack from Alexander, at the Battle of Issus in 333 BC. This **mosaic** is thought to be a copy made by a Roman artist in the 1st century BC of a Greek-style wall painting which is now lost.

Face of fallen Persian reflected in his shield

King Darius of Persia

Charioteer desperately tries to turn the king's chariot round

Persian cavalry

Province of Rome

By about 278 BC the empire had split into three major kingdoms – Egypt, Syria and Babylonia, and Macedonia. Many of the old city-states continued to flourish. This was the start of what is known as the Hellenistic Age (from the word *Hellen*, which is what the Greeks called themselves). It saw the spread of Greek culture through Persia to India and north Africa. In return, new influences transformed Greek art. Palaces were decorated in an oriental (Eastern) manner. Sculpture began to include Egyptian myths and styles, and the Greeks learned to make blown-glass objects.

The Hellenistic Age was ended by the rise of a new and much stronger Mediterranean power – Rome. The Romans defeated Macedonia and destroyed Corinth in 146 BC, making Greece part of its growing **empire**. The great ages of Greece were over.

▼ The Stoa of Attalos stood in the Agora of Athens. It was originally built by King Attalos in about 140 BC, but was later destroyed by fire. Between 1952 and 1956 the Stoa was carefully reconstructed using some ancient materials.

The spread of Greek culture

Greek ideas, science, language and religion influenced and changed society in the Near East for more than a thousand years. New Greek cities, such Alexandria in Egypt, Antioch in Syria and Pergamum in Asia Minor, were magnificently laid out with terraces, colonnades, market places and vast temples.

Sculpture became more ornate and realistic, and featured famous works such as the Winged Victory of Samothrace and the Venus de Milo (the Greek goddess Aphrodite), shown on the left. Elaborate jewellery was produced, as well as moulded glass, wall paintings and **mosaics**.

Open galleries with columns

Church built when Greece became part of the Byzantine Empire

Upper colonnade

Ruins of Classical buildings of the Agora

Architecture

From about 550 BC, a grand kind of Greek architecture appeared. Where previously buildings had been built of timber, bricks and plain stones, massive temples of limestone and marble were now built. There were shrines for the god of each city-state – to Zeus at Olympia, Artemis at Ephesus, Apollo at Didyma. Other monumental public buildings were theatres, market courts and assembly halls.

Building a temple

A Greek temple is rectangular, with regular straight sides and square corners. There was no other way to do it. At this time, no one had learned to build rounded arches or vaults, so the roof was simply made by laying beams on top of vertical walls or **columns**. Nevertheless, the Greek style was majestic. Carved columns stood on a stepped stone base. Above them was the horizontal ceiling, and above that the pitched roof.

Marble for the temples had to be dug and transported from the quarry, then cut to size and carved by craftsmen using iron tools. The blocks were raised into place and fixed together with **bronze** or iron pins. Finally, the erected stones were decorated, which meant polishing the marble, tiling the floor, and **gilding** and colouring statues and paintings.

Who paid for all this? A temple was a public place, so the cost of building it was usually met by the taxes levied on the state's citizens, on foreigners and on imported goods. Sometimes wealthy individuals also gave money for these works.

▼ The Athenians built the small Temple of Athena Nike ('victorious') on the Acropolis in 421 BC to celebrate their defeat of the Persians.

Sculptural frieze showing an assembly of the gods

Sculptural frieze depicting the Battle of Marathon

Fluted columns with Ionic capitals

Inner room or cella, for cult statue

Temple built from local Pentelic marble

Lost Wonder

One of the most amazing of all Greek buildings is no longer standing, but we know about it through the descriptions of Greek and Roman writers, and also the much later work of archaeologists. The Mausoleum at Halicarnassus in Asia Minor, built in about 353 BC, was one of the **Seven Wonders of the World**. It was a magnificent tomb, 41 metres high, and had three storeys – a basement, a colonnade and then a pyramid. On top of all this was a large statue. The Mausoleum was destroyed in an earthquake.

The Parthenon

The temple of the Parthenon is on the highest point of the Acropolis. Work on it began in 447 BC and took nine years to complete. The temple was dedicated to Athena, goddess of wisdom and warfare, and patron of Athens.

Columns and capitals

Carved columns and horizontal **lintels** are the classic Greek style. Greek columns were not all the same, but had three main styles, or orders. The Doric order is the simplest, with heavy proportions and little decoration. The Ionic is slimmer, with a ram's horn pattern at the top (**capital**). This one (left) is decorated with two pairs of *volutes* (spiral carved ornaments in the shape of rams' horns). The Corinthian has an even more elaborate capital, decorated with carved leaves.

▼ The Parthenon originally contained a huge statue of the goddess Athena, 12 metres high, made of ivory and gold.

Columns of creamy-white marble, from quarries at nearby Mt Penteli

Inner marble walls, also with a frieze

The roof was once covered in marble tiles

The pediment, where there were once sculptures showing scenes from mythology and Athenian history

A carved **frieze** stretched for nearly 160 m around the entire building

Steps running all round give a rectangular base to the building

Inside the city-state

Ancient Greece had no capital city. The city-states of the Greek world were fiercely independent, and frequently fighting each other. The stronger ones conquered the weaker ones, taking over their trade, and forcing them to provide money and troops for more wars. Several states became very powerful in this way (Corinth, Thebes, Samos and Syracuse in Sicily), but after the Persian Wars two of them – Athens and Sparta – dominated all the others.

Inside Athens

Athens is the most famous example of an ancient **democracy**. The city ruled itself through a government which was elected by its own citizens and bound by its own laws. Citizens were free to give their views at the Assembly, which met at least once a week, and put forward a motion. If this was passed, it became law. Daily running of affairs was in the hands of the Council of 500 citizens, who were chosen by lot once a year. Nobody could serve as councillor for more than two years.

Even so, Athens was not like a modern democracy. A 'citizen' had to be male, adult and Athenian: women, slaves and foreigners were not allowed to vote or take public office. Nor were citizens always allowed complete freedom of speech. In 399 BC the great philosopher Socrates was put to death (by being forced to drink poison), because things he had said were thought to have undermined the religion and morality of the state.

▼ This marble **relief carving** of Athena, the patron goddess of Athens, was commissioned as a 'votive' (religious dedication) for the Acropolis.

Helmet and spear: Athena was often shown in armour to illustrate her love of battle

Athena reads a list of citizens killed in battle, which is inscribed on this stone

She wears a peplos, a garment made from a folded rectangle of woollen cloth

Inside Sparta

Spartan society was organized in a very different way, as a mixture of democracy and monarchy. It had two kings, who sat on the state's governing council along with 28 elders chosen by the citizens.

Sparta's main business was war. There was no time to create grand buildings or paint pottery, and comparatively few Spartan works of art have been discovered. Manual work was done by slaves called *helots*, who were mostly inhabitants of a conquered neighbour, Messenia. This left the Spartans free to concentrate on a rigorous system of military training.

Spartan babies were inspected at birth, and the weakest were left to die on an exposed hillside. At the age of seven the boys were assembled in packs and taught toughness and obedience, playing naked and barefoot. At twenty they became full soldiers of the state. Girls were encouraged to exercise as fully as the boys, but they did not fight. Their job was to produce more Spartan children.

▼ This bronze statue of a boxer, made in the Ist century BC, is a Roman copy of a Greek original. It is slightly bigger than life-size to emphasize the boxer's power.

Weary battle-scarred face with broken nose and battered ears

Bindings on forearms and hands to protect them during a fight

Portraits in stone

Greek sculptors wanted to create beautiful forms, so they showed people looking as perfect as possible, with noble faces. But from about 400 BC some artists tried to capture the real personality of their subject. A head of Socrates, for example, depicts a lively, intelligent but ugly man. An ivory carving of Philip of Macedonia shows that he had lost an eye.

Trade and warfare

The mountainous landscape of Greece made overland transport very difficult. So it was by sea that Greek settlers explored the Mediterranean. They built up trading links with ports as far apart as southern Spain and north Africa. Trade brought wealth to Greece, and helped spread Hellenic culture.

Traders were looking for goods that were not found in Greece. Some went to Syracuse and southern Italy because of the rich agricultural land. Other sailors bought huge supplies of grain from the shores of the Black Sea. Settlers from the west coast of Asia Minor founded Massilia (now Marseilles) in southern France, where they could buy tin and other vital metals.

The port of Piraeus

Attica, the area around Athens, was one of Greece's largest communities from about 450 BC. Its large population (roughly 150,000, plus about 100,000 slaves) needed a huge and regular supply of food, most of which had to be **imported**. Almost all goods bound for Attica came through the port of Piraeus, a short distance from Athens. Corn, slaves, timber, iron, copper and luxury items such as scents from Egypt arrived. Meanwhile the locally produced exports – olive oil, wine, pottery, silver and carvings – were loaded up to be sold abroad. Bankers set up shop in the long colonnades which lined the harbour, ready to buy, sell or lend money for business ventures.

The fishmonger cuts up a fish on his counter

Fish head on floor

◄ Greek traders and settlers spread around the Mediterranean. This Greek vase was made in Southern Italy in the 4th century BC.

Comic depiction of a talkative customer

Soldiers and their weapons

In order to keep hold of these valuable trade routes, the Greeks often had to go to war – against each other and against rival trading nations. We know a lot about the soldiers and their fighting methods because they were frequently pictured on pottery and in sculpture and relief carvings. Greeks saw battle as a noble and heroic activity, and an ideal subject for art.

The most effective warrior was the hoplite, a heavily armed infantry soldier. His face and head were protected by a plumed bronze helmet, and he wore **bronze** armour on his upper body and legs. Hoplites carried a wooden shield with a bronze rim to prevent splitting, and fought with a long jabbing spear and a short sword. Most armies also had troops of archers and slingers, as well as giant catapults for damaging city walls.

▼ The power of the Greek city-states was often based on their armies. This vase from 7th century Corinth shows a battle between two hoplite forces.

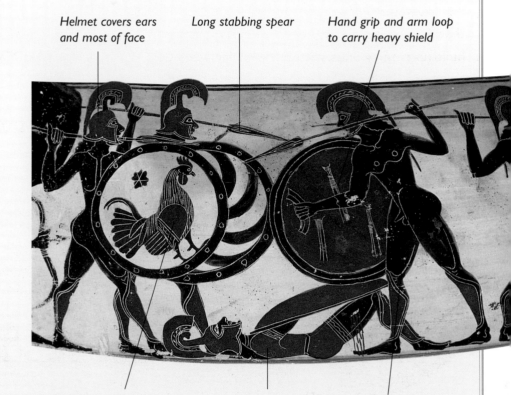

Helmet covers ears and most of face

Long stabbing spear

Hand grip and arm loop to carry heavy shield

Shield with cockerel emblem, probably a personal motif

Fallen hoplite

Warriors shown nude to indicate their heroic status

Braving the seas

Cargo ships were often clumsy and slow because of their large rounded holds for grain or other goods. They had one big square sail, which made them hard to steer. There were no compasses or maps, so ships stayed within sight of land and anchored at night. This 8th century BC vase, decorated in the Geometric style, shows an illustration of a Greek warship. You can just make out the lines of rowers and soldiers. The fastest Greek ships were **triremes** – speedy, narrow warships, built with a copper ram in the bow. Driven forward by 170 oarsmen who sat in three tiers, a trireme aimed to ram an enemy ship and make a hole below the waterline.

A world of colour

The great sculptor Praxiteles was once asked which of his statues he liked best. He replied, 'Those which Nikias painted.' We are so used to seeing plain Greek sculptures in museums, that it is a surprise to realize that many Greek sculptures were originally coloured. Artists used paints, **gilding,** stones and copper to make the figures look more lifelike. Temples and other buildings were also decorated with bright colours.

We do not see Greek art as the Greeks saw it, when it was part of a living, vibrant **civilization**. We are used to thinking of plain white marble, or dull red bronze statues which are usually broken or incomplete in some way. The Venus de Milo has no arms, the Nike of Samothrace has no head, and most warriors have their spears and shields missing. The Greek buildings that remain are at least partly in ruins, and the more important fragments have been taken away to exhibit in museums, with special lighting and spacing.

Originally, of course, all these things were complete, coloured in vibrant red, silver and gold, and made to look as lifelike as possible. They were not simply things to look at, but had a definite purpose. The sculptures and temples were created for the sake of religion and politics – not art – and they were not meant to be seen in museums.

The Nike's head has never been found

Wings held back as the figure alights on board

Clothing swept back by forward movement

▶ Headless but still magnificent, the Nike (also called the Winged Victory) of Samothrace is depicted landing on the bow of a warship, with swirling clothes to show movement. The sculpture was originally mounted on a fountain to commemorate a sea victory.

Adding colour

Artists were colouring their statues as far back as the 6th century BC. They rubbed wax paints on to marble carvings to give different shades for hair, eyes, lips and clothing. Very little of this kind of paint can now be seen as it has faded or been cleaned away. However, we can get an idea of how vivid the colours were by looking at clay figures and vases from the same period, where the **pigments** are preserved by firing.

Much more original colouring, using metals and stones, has survived on bronze statues. The teeth were inlaid with silver, and the lips and nipples with copper. Eyes were made of stone, either whole pieces or crushed and made into a paste, and then coloured.

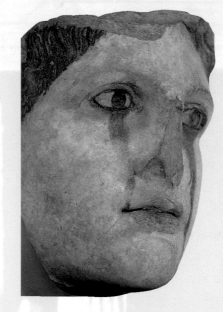

▲ Detail of a marble statue showing how the face was painted.

Three great sculptors

Pheidias (worked c.465 to c.425 BC) was renowned for his architecture and painting as well as his sculpture. He was in charge of designing and producing the statues and relief decoration for the Parthenon.

Praxiteles (worked c.375 to c.330 BC) was skilled at conveying the emotion of his subjects in marble. This made him the most famous of Athenian artists. However, hardly any of his work has survived, though several copies by later artists can still be seen. The carved stone head of the goddess Aphrodite shown below is believed to be the work of pupils or followers of Praxiteles.

Lysippos (worked c.340 to c.320 BC) became the official sculptor for Alexander the Great (who decreed that no one else should be allowed to make his statue). He was famed for his ability to capture bodies in action. None of his 1500 bronze figures has survived.

◄ Beautiful marble carving of the goddess Aphrodite, 325 BC, from the school of Praxiteles.

Graceful and gently sculpted facial features, for which Praxiteles was noted

Sensuous mouth: Aphrodite was the goddess of love

Visionaries and thinkers

The ancient Greeks were among the earliest people to examine the world around them with a view to understanding its nature and the principles that govern it. Early Greek ideas about mathematics and science were far ahead of anything that had been achieved elsewhere in the world, and underpinned scientific, mathematical and philosophical progress for many centuries to come.

The power of words

The Greeks had no newspapers or television. There was no printing, so books had to be copied by hand on rolls of **papyrus**. This made them very expensive, and though there were several libraries (notably the one at Alexandria in Egypt, which by about 250 BC boasted nearly half a million texts), very few people owned a book. The spoken word was therefore very important.

One famous philosopher, Socrates, encouraged others to think about moral questions. He did not preach a specific philosophy, but asked questions, hoping that people would realize how ignorant they were. Socrates explored his ideas through discussions, but did not write them down.

▲ A sheet of manuscript from the 2nd century AD, which is part of the only surviving book made of papyrus.

◀ The philosopher Plato is shown talking with his pupils in this Roman **mosaic** from a house in Pompeii (the Italian city buried by the eruption of Vesuvius in AD 79).

Lessons held outdoors under trees

Plato in dialogue with his pupils

It was Plato, another great philosopher, who wrote down many of Socrates' ideas in the form of conversations, or 'dialogues', between teacher and pupils.

Herodotus, known as 'the Father of History', did not simply record facts like the chroniclers before him. In his massive history of the Persian Wars he looked at different stories about past events and attempted to explain why they happened.

Epics and lyrics

The first great works of Greek literature started as spoken stories. The **epic** poems *The Iliad* and *The Odyssey*, believed to have been written by Homer at the end of the Dark Ages, were based on tales that had been recited from memory over at least two centuries by skilled storytellers. *The Iliad* narrates episodes from the Trojan Wars, and *The Odyssey* tells of the long journey home of Odysseus, one of the Greeks at Troy. Incidents from the poems were favourite subjects for sculptors and vase painters.

More personal poetry developed all over the Greek world from about 650 BC. Poets wrote about their loves, hates, adventures and drinking parties, but much of this verse has disappeared. The great female poet Sappho, who lived on the island of Lesbos, is known only through one complete poem and a handful of fragments. On the other hand, the Theban writer Pindar left four entire books of **odes**.

Set in stone

Ancient Greek letters probably developed from the alphabet of the Phoenicians of north Africa, which had 22 symbols. The earliest Greek texts found by **archaeologists** are scratched on pieces of pottery from about 725 BC. The arrival of writing meant that financial accounts, chronicles and laws could be recorded on stone tablets.

▶ This inscription from the 2nd century AD shows details of a civic decree about the collection of taxes by city officials. Texts like these give us vital first-hand information about ancient Greece.

Early Greek letters were square, straight figures, suitable for carving with chisel and mallet. Later, many letters became more rounded and simple, as a result of being written in ink.

There were 24 letters in the ancient Greek alphabet, each with its traditional name. The alphabet was adopted by Athens and much of Greece in about 402 BC.

Everyday life

The warm climate meant that Greeks spent most of their lives outdoors. Houses were not grand and imposing places like the temples and other public buildings. They were usually built around an open courtyard, with a well or covered water tank in the middle. The walls were made of mud bricks baked in the sun, and they had small windows that were covered with wooden shutters to keep out the heat.

Family life went on inside these simple homes. The rooms were not very large, except in rich households. The biggest and smartest was the dining room, used by the men only, which might have a **mosaic** floor and comfortable couches. There were also work rooms, where the women did the weaving and cooking. The floors here would be plain stone or even beaten earth. Furniture was simple – a few wooden chairs, stools, tables and storage chests. Many of these items are pictured on vases.

◀ This red-figure pottery painting shows a scene from the interior of a Greek house.

Woman holding **bronze** mirror

High-backed chair with fabric covers

Doorway to a bedroom

A woman's place

The men of the household went out every day – to work or to talk with other men in the city. The women spent most of their time indoors, and had very little independence. Marriages were usually arranged by parents, and after this women were under their husband's authority. They could not vote or own property. Sparta was the exception, where women lived much freer lives: they were allowed to own property and, although they could not vote, their views were listened to.

Housework kept women very busy, although most families had at least one slave to do the hardest jobs. There was cleaning to do, as well as grinding grain and making bread, fetching water, buying provisions and cooking. Spinning woollen yarn and weaving cloth was important work, making things both to use and to sell.

Greek children

If a baby was born sickly or deformed, it might have a very short life – put into a jar and left out to die in a lonely place. A healthy baby was a cause of great joy in the household. Paintings and clay models show that young children had plenty of toys and games to play: dolls, rattles, spinning tops and swings. Children also had pets, including hares, tortoises and dogs. Boys went to school at the age of seven. Schools were private but not expensive, and there pupils learned to read, write and play music as well as the basic skills of boxing, wrestling and athletics. Girls, as always, stayed at home.

Clothes

Most Greeks wore a very simple tunic called a *chiton*, which was a rectangular piece of linen cloth wrapped round the body and fixed with a brooch or belt. In winter, they also put on a kind of cloak called a *himation*, which was another square of cloth, this time made of wool. On their feet were sandals, though in summer they might go barefoot. The clay figure (right) shows a woman wearing a *peplos*.

The ends of the peplos are pinned at the shoulders

The waist is fastened with a belt

To shorten the garment, some of the length is pulled up to hang over the belt

The rectangle of cloth is wrapped around the wearer under the arms

Vase painting

We can learn more about ancient Greece from its pottery than almost any other source, partly because there is a lot of it! You might think other art forms would survive better over 2000 years, but in fact bronze from statues can be melted down and reused, and stone from statues and buildings can be broken up and reused, but a broken vase can only be thrown away and left… for archaeologists to find and put back together. The pictures painted on vases show us a staggering variety of scenes, from athletics, battles and episodes from **mythology** to simple everyday activities like weaving and winemaking.

▼ A *krater* (bowl for mixing wine and water) from the Geometric period.

Pair of horses depicted as almost one animal, with eight legs and two heads and tails

How vase painting developed

- **Geometric**

  The first great style of decoration began in around 875 BC. It featured geometric shapes, such as straight lines, triangles and zigzags, painted in bands round the pot. Simple stick-figures of humans and animals were painted inside these complex patterns.

- **Black-figure**

  This technique was developed in Corinth in about 720 BC. Painters showed people in much more detail, and began to tell stories in their illustrations. They used black paint for these figures and scratched lines to show details. Later, they also used red and white colouring.

- **Red-figure**

  Around 525 BC, Athenian artists invented a clever new process. Instead of painting black figures, they used the black for the background, and left the figures blank (showing the natural red of the clay). This allowed them to add much more delicate detail to the figures, and make them more rounded and life-like.

Charioteers are carrying round shields with semi-circular cut-outs on either side

Both chariot wheels are shown

Potters and painters

Clay was one of the most useful and flexible materials in the ancient world. Greeks needed clay pots for everything from storing oil and wine to carrying water and using as prizes. There were potteries in nearly every town or village. Of course, ordinary people used plain, everyday pots, but some pots were beautifully decorated as ornaments or for use in religious ceremonies.

During the 5th century BC, Athens became the centre for making high-quality painted vases. The craftsmen worked in the Karameikos, or potter's quarter of the city. At this time a few also began to sign their work – either as the maker or the painter (and some did both). Very little is known about these wonderful artists. By careful study, modern scholars can identify the work of some painters, even when there is no signature. These are simply known by the place where the vase was found or the subjects painted on them, such as 'The Gorgon Painter' and 'The Achilles Painter'.

Chariot moves towards the viewer

Red colour used for clothing

▲ A *krater* from the Attic region in the black-figure style, showing a chariot drawn by horses.

Using the evidence of pottery

Pottery was made in almost every region of Greece. Each area had its own local styles and shapes, and by studying which styles are found in different places we can build up a picture of how far goods were transported for trade. The age of a pot can also be worked out by examining how it was decorated.

◀ An Attic cup from about 490 BC in the red-figure style. The illustration shows an episode from Homer's *Iliad*, with the slave girl Briseis and Phoenix, friend of Achilles.

Playing games

Many Greeks were rich enough to employ slaves to do most of the work, so they had plenty of spare time and they spent some of it playing games. Greek painters and sculptors have left images of several of these, including ball games, board games, knucklebones, and a curious game called kottabos which involved flicking the dregs of your wine at a target. Although kottabos was played by men at drinking parties, other games were enjoyed by adults and children alike.

Knucklebones is shown on several vases and sculptures. It was popular because all you needed were five ankle bones from small, cloven-footed animals. The game involved throwing and catching the bones in various different ways, like the modern game of jacks. For example, the player could throw up the first bone, pick up another while it was in the air, and then catch the first bone as it came down. A second stage was played by throwing two bones up in the air while picking up a third, and so on.

Children's games

Games with hoops and tops were popular amongst young children. They played ball games, including one with a stick and ball that looks similar to hockey. Paintings also show a game of piggyback, in which a blindfolded child has to find her way to a set point while carrying one of her friends.

▼ A game of knucklebones is played by the two girls in this sculpture. It is not clear from the statuette which stage the game has reached – they may be about to place the bones on the ground, ready to play.

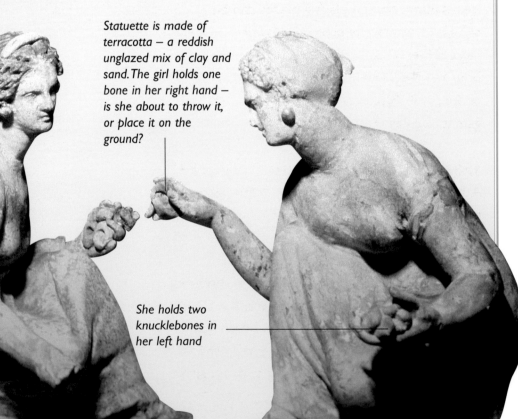

Statuette is made of terracotta – a reddish unglazed mix of clay and sand. The girl holds one bone in her right hand – is she about to throw it, or place it on the ground?

She holds two knucklebones in her left hand

Board games

The ancient Greeks played board games, but we do not know much about them. One writer describes a game called five lines, a kind of noughts and crosses played on a board with counters. One of the best pieces of artistic evidence for board-game playing is a vase painting (right) by Exekias, a mid-6th century Athenian artist famous for his black-figure vase decoration. It shows the heroes Achilles and Ajax playing a board game. The two men are in armour, and they are presumably playing during a quiet period in the Trojan Wars.

Vase painters portrayed their subjects from the side, in profile. This means that this vase provides good evidence of the two heroes' clothes and armour, but it is impossible to see the board. In spite of this, the painting does give us some information. No tall playing pieces can be seen, so the game is probably played with flat counters. Both men are reaching for the board at the same time, so the game is likely to be played quickly, unlike elaborate strategy games such as chess.

Games in Athens and Sparta

Athens and Sparta had different attitudes to game playing. In Athens there are many pictures showing people taking part in sport, but there is also plenty of evidence that the Athenians enjoyed pastimes like board games and knucklebones. The Spartans, however, emphasized fitness above all and went in for sports like running and wrestling rather than board games. In Sparta girls as well as boys took part in these sports, but when Athenian artists showed girls relaxing, they were usually playing games like knucklebones.

Both figures hold their spears, suggesting that this is a quick game played during a lull in fighting

Ajax leans forward to move a counter

Flat playing surface

▲ The two heroes Achilles and Ajax play a board game on this vase, which is painted in the black-figure style. The vase is a rounded type that **archaeologists** call a 'belly amphora' and was used for the storage of grain, oil or wine.

Eating and drinking

The warm, dry climate of Greece made it easy to grow some crops. Greek farmers produced barley and wheat as well as olives, figs and nuts. They dug up the soil with ploughs drawn by oxen or, if they had no animals, they used spades and hoes. However, most of Greece is mountainous and has little flat and fertile land. Flocks of sheep and goats could be grazed here, but little could be grown. As their populations increased, many city-states had to **import** vital stocks of grain from settlements in Italy and near the Black Sea.

Rich and poor

The Greeks ate little during the day. A snack of olives or fruit at sunrise might be followed by a light lunch at midday (or nothing at all). The main meal was eaten at sunset after the day's work was done. For poor people, this usually meant beans or barley, which was soaked and made into soup or a kind of paste which was mixed with spices and baked. The lucky ones had plenty of olives, cheese and fruit to go with it, while many kept hens to provide them with eggs.

Only richer people could afford to buy fish or meat regularly, and this was usually roasted on a spit over an open fire. The rich also ate bread made from wheat flour, which was finer and more expensive than barley flour. There was no sugar, so food was sweetened with honey, which became an important crop. The honey-bee colonies were kept in hives made of wood, reeds or even clay.

▼ This black-figure vase, made in Athens in about 520 BC, shows a scene from country life.

Climbing into the tree to reach the high branches

One farmer picks up the fallen olives

Farmers use sticks to knock down olives from the tree

Hunting and fishing

In ancient times, woodland still covered much of the hills and mountains. There were many wild animals, such as boar and deer, and hunting them was a good way of putting meat in the cooking pot. Greeks hunted on foot with spears and bows, though they also caught game in snares and nets. We know this from many illustrations on mosaics and painted pottery.

The sea was an even more important source of tasty food. Many fishing boats worked along Greece's long coastline, bringing in a great variety of fish including tuna, red mullet, octopus and anchovies. These were sold fresh or pickled in salt to keep them through the winter. Poor people made their soup taste more exciting by putting in small amounts of salted fish.

▶ The painting on this plate shows a huntsman returning home with his dog, carrying the hares he has caught.

A drinking party

A Greek dinner party was called a *symposium*, which means 'drinking together'. We know a lot about these events from many written descriptions, and from painted vases, such as this red-figure-style painting from an amphora. The men ate and drank while lying on couches. The wine was mixed with water in a special large vessel called a *krater* and then served out by slave boys. The women present tended to be slaves or courtesans.

All wear woollen bands around their heads   A slave boy brings wine

A woman entertains the group with music

The men recline on elaborate couches with plenty of cushions

Dish of snacks

Theatre and the Olympic Games

Jagged edge of marble probably copies the broken Greek original

Some of the most spectacular buildings that remain from ancient Greece are the theatres – vast auditoriums, such as the 14,000-seat Theatre at Epidauros. At Delphi there are remains of the Olympic stadium, which seated 7000 spectators.

The ancient Greeks invented the theatre and the Olympic Games, but unlike plays and sports today these events were not held simply to amuse people. They were usually part of much bigger religious festivals, organized to please the gods and bring peace and prosperity. Each city had its own festivals throughout the year, when the whole population took a holiday to enjoy the excitement of the occasion.

Greek drama

Greek theatre probably started in about 550 BC, in the songs and dances performed in honour of Dionysos, the god of wine. In Athens this developed into a four-day drama festival called the Dionysia, in which processions and sacrifices were followed by as many as five different plays each day. Fifth-century Athens produced some of the greatest playwrights of all time, including Aeschylus and Sophocles (who wrote tragedies) and Aristophanes (who wrote comedies), whose work is still performed today.

All the people on stage were men, who wore masks over their faces. Most of them formed the **chorus**, who commented on events in the play but did not take part in the action. Scenery and costumes were often lavish, and prizes were given to the best writers, producers and actors.

▼ A marble bust of the playwright Sophocles. This is a Roman copy of a Greek original from the 4th century BC, now lost.

Plinth or base statue

The Olympic Games

Many religious festivals involved athletic competitions. The biggest and most famous of these were the Olympic Games, which were first held in 776 BC at Olympia in honour of Zeus, father of the gods, who was believed to live on Mount Olympus. Weeks beforehand, heralds throughout Greece announced the games, and warring states called a truce so that people could travel safely.

The five-day Games began with sacrifices to Zeus and other ceremonies, and then the competition got under way with a race between chariots pulled by four horses. Then came more horse races and the pentathlon (wrestling, long-jump, discus, javelin and 200 metres race). There were boxing and *pankration* (all-out fighting) contests, as well as long-distance running races and even a race in which the competitors wore armour. Only the winner got a prize — a wreath of olive leaves.

A runner practising his starting position

Each wrestler tries to get a firm grip on his opponent's arms, ready to throw him

▲ A marble relief carving of athletes wrestling, originally produced to adorn the base of a statue in Athens in about 510 BC.

A night at the theatre

Nearly every Greek city had a theatre. One of the most famous was at Epidauros. It was a huge open-air structure with 54 tiers of seats set into a semi-circle in the hillside. It was so perfectly built that an actor speaking in a normal voice could be heard on the very top tier. People probably brought cushions to put on the stone seating (which was hollowed out below so they could tuck their legs in), and food and wine to keep them going during the performance, which lasted several hours. The vast bowl of the Theatre of Epidauros was originally built as part of a sanctuary dedicated to Asclepius, the god of healing.

Religion and mythology

Religion occupied a central place in the lives of the ancient Greeks. They believed that the gods controlled all aspects of their lives. If these gods became angry, they would send disaster and bad luck. So the Greeks worked hard to please them, with prayers and **sacrifices**, elaborate festivals and grand temples.

The gods might be frightening, but they were not beasts or monsters. The Greeks saw them as looking just like humans, sometimes moving among ordinary people and taking part in their daily lives. They had the same feelings and faults, although they never grew old or lost their strength. Much of what we know about Greek **mythology** comes from statues. Sculptors and painters showed the gods and goddesses as ideal beings, perfect and beautiful. The many stories about them form the basis of Greek myths.

The family of gods

There were a bewildering number of gods, but the twelve most important ones lived on Mount Olympus, the highest mountain in Greece.

Zeus, the king of the gods, was the most powerful of the gods and ruled the skies, sending fine weather or storms. When he was angry, he would hurl his deadly thunderbolts.

Hera, Zeus's wife, was the goddess of children and marriage. She often quarrelled with Zeus about his love affairs with other women.

Poseidon, Zeus's brother, was god of the sea. He drove a chariot through the waters, drawn by foaming white horses, and his weapon was a trident.

▼ The Greek gods have inspired countless artists since **Classical** times. This statue of Poseidon was carved in marble by Lambert-Sigisbert Adam in 1757.

Thick beard and wild hair

A trident, Poseidon's main symbol

Poseidon is always shown bare-chested

At his feet, a triton (a minor sea god) hands him a piece of coral.

▲ A vast ceiling painting of the gods on a cloudy Mount Olympus, completed in 1528 by the Italian artist Giulio Romano and his assistants.

Demeter was the goddess of farming and crops. When her daughter was kidnapped by Hades, she made the earth barren until the girl was released, and then restored fertility. This explained the different seasons of the year.

Hestia was goddess of the home and hearth. Many Greeks kept a fire burning in her honour.

Athena, a daughter of Zeus, was goddess of wisdom and warfare, arts and crafts, and patron goddess of Athens.

Apollo was god of light and music. The best loved of all the gods, he also was also associated with archery, medicine and prophecy (foretelling the future).

Artemis was goddess of the moon and hunting. Twin sister of Apollo, she spent her time in the woods of Arcadia, hunting wild animals with her hounds.

Hermes was the messenger of the gods. He conducted dead people to the Underworld. Hermes was also a trickster who loved to tell lies and could make himself invisible.

Aphrodite was goddess of beauty and love. One of Zeus's many daughters, she was born out of the sea-foam washed up on the shore.

Hephaestos was god of metal crafts and fire, who knew how to make many magical objects, including a gold watchdog for Zeus.

Ares was god of war. He was not popular with the other gods, because he represented the rage and violence of warfare.

▶ The black-figure painting on this amphora shows the goddess Demeter, Persephone and Triptolemus.

Triptolemus, teacher of the skills of agriculture, on his magical wheeled throne

The goddess Demeter and Persephone, her daughter

Festivals and oracles

The aim of Greek religion was to please the gods. This meant sacrifices and festivals and elaborate ceremonies, to make the gods happy and friendly towards the mortals. If the correct rituals were performed, the gods would send bumper harvests, or victory in war, or other good things. If the gods were neglected, they might send storms, defeat and all kinds of disasters.

People made sure that the gods also looked after their homes and families. Outside the front door they kept a small statue of Hermes (to guard against burglars), while inside a fire burned in the hearth to honour Hestia. In the courtyard there was usually an altar to Zeus as protector and defender of the household.

Public religion

Every city and village had its calendar of religious festivals. In Athens there were more than 60 throughout the year. These ranged from huge ceremonies, with games, dancing and even beauty contests, to much smaller celebrations for a local god within a tribe or family. Greeks looked forward to these events as holidays and a time to enjoy themselves together.

▲ The sanctuary of Apollo at Delphi was thought to be the centre (or navel) of the world. It was marked by this mysterious *omphalos* stone, shaped like a navel or an egg, which stood on the esplanade outside the temple. The marble is carved with wreaths.

The biggest festivals were for people from all over the Greek world, and celebrated the major gods. Zeus was honoured at the Games at Olympia and Nemea (where the victors won crowns of celery). The Pythian Games at Delphi were dedicated to Apollo and included musical competitions. The Isthmian Games at Corinth were in honour of Poseidon. All of these meetings featured sacrifices and solemn prayers.

◄ A musical competition depicted on a vase made in about 510 BC.

Judges, carrying staves to show their official function

A perfomer mounts the stage

The work of a priest

The council of the city-state elected the priests for a city's temples – usually men for the male gods, and women for the female ones. They conducted the religious rituals, and were expected to know proper words and actions for the ceremonies. On top of this, they were responsible for the upkeep of the building, whitewashing the walls and making repairs.

Another important religious figure was the prophet or seer. Their job was to explain the meaning of omens and how they showed what would happen in the future. An omen could be anything from a dream to the flight of a bird, but only a prophet could correctly interpret what it meant. Some of them told the future by inspecting the insides of sacrificial animals.

Consulting the oracle

In special circumstances, the gods would answer questions about the future asked by worshippers. This could be done at sacred sites called **oracles**. There were several oracles throughout Greece, including the famous sanctuary of Apollo at Delphi. At the Dodona oracle in Epiros, people wrote their questions on lead tablets, and received the answers in the sound of the wind in a sacred oak tree.

▼The *tholos* at the sanctuary of Athena at ancient Delphi. This graceful circular monument once had 20 Doric **columns**. Nobody knows exactly what it was used for.

Bases of outer ring of columns

Three columns re-erected in 1938

Circular platform of tholos building

Heroes and heroines

Greeks loved and honoured their heroes almost as much as their gods. These may once have been real people, but they had been turned into legends as demi-gods, or beings halfway between humans and gods. The Greeks believed that they had been born as ordinary mortals, but became godlike because they performed great deeds of strength or courage. However, in the end they would die and go to the Underworld.

Tales about heroes and heroines were passed down by storytellers. Many of them became cult figures, who were worshipped with special ceremonies at local shrines. The Greeks saw heroes as examples to copy, and also as people who might help them communicate with the true gods. All the same, not all heroes were completely heroic. There were many imperfect and vulnerable characters who acted in ways which were very human.

Herakles

The most famous of all the mythical heroes, even today, is Herakles or Hercules. The original Herakles was possibly a leader in Mycenaean times, but over the centuries he was turned into a hero. People believed he was the son of Zeus and a mortal woman. He was enormously strong. The story goes that when he was just a baby in his cradle, he strangled two snakes sent to kill him.

Herakles is best known for the Twelve Labours (tasks) he had to complete. These amazing deeds included killing the Nemean Lion with his bare hands, destroying the man-eating Stymphalian Birds and capturing the three-headed guard dog of the Underworld.

▶ For his second Labour, Herakles had to kill the poisonous water snake called the Hydra, which kept growing new heads whenever he chopped one off. The **Renaissance** artist Giambologna created this bronze in the 16th century AD.

Sculpture shows a club, though in legend Herakles killed the Hydra with his sword

One of the Hydra's nine heads

Clawed serpent's feet

Theseus and the Minotaur

Theseus was the national hero of Athens, and the son of either Aegeus (King of Athens) or the god Poseidon. He had many adventures showing his daring and strength, though he is best remembered for his voyage to Crete. His mission was to find and kill the Minotaur, a monster that was half-man and half-bull and lived in an underground maze called the Labyrinth. Theseus was helped by Ariadne, a Cretan princess, who gave him a ball of thread which he unwound as he made his way into the Labyrinth. Having slain the Minotaur, he found his way out again by following the thread. He sailed away with Ariadne (though he later abandoned her) and became King of Athens.

Monsters of myth

Artists loved to depict the many weird beasts that appear in the Greek myths. Many of them are mixtures of more than one animal. Medusa the Gorgon was a mortal woman, whose hair was made of writhing snakes and whose face was so horrible that anyone who saw it was turned to stone. The Hydra had the body of a dog and nine snake-like heads which grew back double when chopped off. The fire-breathing Chimera had the head of a lion, the body of a goat and the tail of a snake. This 6th-century BC black-figure vase shows Theseus fighting the Minotaur in the Labyrinth.

Theseus wrestles with the monster

Ariadne watches the fight

Minotaur with bull's head

Marble and bronze

Greek sculptors had several materials to choose from. The earliest carvers probably made statues of wood, but these rotted and none has been found. Some used clay, but this was only suitable for small pieces as it broke easily. Stone and **bronze** statues were stronger and lasted far longer, even though they were much more expensive and time consuming to produce.

The main purpose of Greek sculpture was religious. City governments or rich citizens paid for the works, which were put on display in sanctuaries and temples and dedicated to the gods. One of the greatest of all these statues, the massive bronze figure of Athena designed by Pheidias, was put up to thank the goddess for the Greek victory over the Persians. Pheidias and other skilled sculptors could ask high fees for such work, and became celebrities.

▶ The *Discus Thrower* is a celebrated portrayal of motion frozen in stillness. This is a marble copy by a Roman artist of the lost bronze sculpture created by Myron in about 450 BC. The original was so highly praised by **Classical** writers that it was copied many times for wealthy Roman buyers.

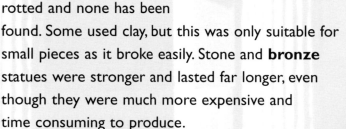

The thrower is caught at the moment between his back-swing and his fore-swing

The discus thrower turns his body as he prepares to launch the discus. Greek sculpture conveys power and emotion in contrast to the stiff poses of Egyptian art.

The tree stump is there to support the heavy marble. It spoils the purity of the statue, and would not have been in Myron's original (lighter) bronze.

Carving stone

A sculptor could take as long as a year to complete a life-size marble statue. He would either do this in his workshop, or travel to where the sculpture was needed. Besides his wages, there was also the cost of quarrying and transporting the block of marble. With all this expense, there was no room for mistakes (even marble will crack and splinter).

First the artist marked the marble block with a grid of lines. Then he sketched the outline of the figure – front, back and sides – on top of this. The grid allowed him to make the proportions match on all four sides. Using his mallet and a rough pointed chisel, he chipped away the excess stone. Once this heavy work had been done, he could use finer tools and then special powders to finish and smooth off the statue.

Casting bronze

To produce a bronze statue, the sculptor had to begin by making a clay model (perhaps built up on a wooden centre). He covered this with a thin coating of wax and placed it inside a mould that was also made of clay. The whole thing was then heated, so that the clay baked hard and the wax melted and ran out. This left a narrow gap between mould and model. Molten bronze was poured in to fill the space, and when it cooled the mould was taken away. The sculptor could now fill in holes or file away rough edges.

Bronze statues were hollow. This made them much lighter than stone. Sculptors were able to make far more delicate pieces, because the thinner parts (such as legs and arms) did not have to support the weight of marble. They could also put weights inside the hollow sections to balance the statue so that it retained its pose.

▼ Bronze head of an unknown god or hero, from the 2nd century BC.

Blank holes for eyes were probably filled with decorated stone

Hollow inside where the original clay model was

43

Timeline

(All BC)

Early history and the Dark Ages (dates approximate)

1600–1200
Mycenaean civilization is at its height

1450
Mycenaeans build palaces at Tiryns, Thebes, Pylos and elsewhere

1220
possible date of the Trojan Wars between Greeks and Troy

1200–1150
Mycenaean sites are destroyed

1100–1000
Dorian people invade Greece

1050
beginning of Greek migration to islands and Asia Minor

Rise of the city-states

875
Geometric pottery begins to be made

776
first Olympic Games are held

750–700
possible dates for writing of Homer's *Iliad* and *Odyssey*

733
Corinth founds Syracuse in Sicily

730
Sparta begins conquest of Messenia

720
development of black-figure vase painting

c.700
first Doric temples built

683
first *archon* (non-royal leader) appointed in Athens

Archaic Age

c.650–510
tyrants rule in Corinth, Miletus, Athens, Samos and other cities

630
first known male nude marble statues are made

621
Draco writes Athens' first code of laws

600
temple of Hera is built at Olympia

c.590
Sappho writing poetry on Lesbos

c.585
first Pythian Games are held at Delphi

546
Persians take control of Ionia

530
Pythagoras (philosopher and mathematician) is active in southern Italy

525
development of red-figure vase painting

498
Pindar is writing poetry in Thebes

490
first Persian invasion of Greek mainland: Greek victory at Marathon

480
second Persian invasion; Battle of Thermopylae; sack of Athens; Greek victory at Salamis

479
Greeks defeat Persians at Plataea

Classical Age

478
Delian League is formed by Greek cities against Persia

c.470
temple of Zeus at Olympia is built

470–430
careers of sculptors Pheidias and Polyclitus, and playwrights Euripides, Sophocles and Aeschylus

461–445
first Peloponnesian War between Athens and Sparta

454

Delian League treasury moves to Athens

447

Parthenon is built in Athens

438

statue of Athena is made for the Parthenon

431–404

second Peloponnesian War

431

Thucydides begins writing his histories

430

statue of Zeus is erected at Olympia

c.430

beginning of Aristophanes' career

429

death of Pericles

420

the temple of Apollo at Bassae is built

415–413

Athenian expedition to Syracuse

404

Athens surrenders to Sparta

401

Greek expedition to Persia

399

death of Socrates

396

beginning of the career of Plato

395–386

war of Sparta against Corinth, Thebes and Argos plus the Persians

371

Thebes defeats Sparta at Leuctra

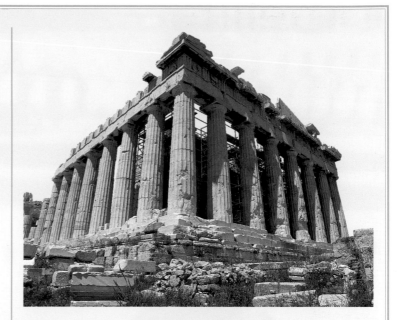

Alexander and the Hellenistic Age

359

Phillip II becomes king of Macedonia

358

theatre at Epidauros is built

356

Alexander the Great is born

353

Mausoleum at Halicarnassus is built

338

Philip defeats Athens and Thebes at Chaeronea

336

death of Philip II

335

Aristotle begins teaching in Athens

334

Alexander leads army into Persia

331

Alexander conquers Egypt and founds Alexandria

326

Alexander reaches the Indus River

323

death of Alexander

295

library is founded at Alexandria

279

Greece is invaded by Gauls

146

sack of Corinth; Greece becomes part of Roman Empire

Glossary

archaeologist person who finds, studies and preserves the remains of ancient civilizations

aristocrat member of class of nobles who ruled in Greece for a period of time

artefact made object, especially a tool, weapon or something used in everyday life

Asia Minor south-western part of Asia (much of modern Turkey)

bronze alloy (mixture) of copper and tin, and sometimes other metals

capital top, decorated section of a column

cast shape molten metal in a mould

chorus in Greek drama, a group of people who speak together, usually commenting on the action of the play

civilization system of social development

Classical to do with the ancient Greeks and Romans, especially their art, architecture and literature

column pillar supporting part of a building, or standing alone as a monument

democracy rule by the people through elected representatives

empire group of countries under the rule of one state

epic long poem telling the story of one or more heroes

frieze horizontal band of sculpture along the upper part of a wall

gild cover with a thin layer of gold

immigrant someone who enters another country to ettle there

import bring in goods from another country

lintel horizontal beam of wood or stone over a door or window

meander pattern of lines which intertwine, used in decoration

mosaic picture or design formed with tiny pieces of coloured stone or glass

mythology body of myths – traditional stories dealing with supernatural beings and happenings, often made up as a way of explaining a country's origins, history and religion

ode poem meant to be sung by a chorus at a Greek play

oracle shrine where ancient Greeks went to ask their gods for advice, or to foretell the future

papyrus early form of paper made from a reed

pigment colouring matter used as paint or dye

politics the art or science of government

relief carving carving that sticks out from a flat background

Renaissance period at the end of the Middle Ages, around the 15th century AD, marked by a revival of interest in the arts and learning of ancient Greece and Rome.

ritual series of actions performed in a religious or other solemn ceremony

sacrifices offerings given to please or honour a god; this often meant the ritual killing of an animal

Seven Wonders of the World seven amazing structures from the ancient world: the pyramids of Egypt, the hanging gardens of Babylon, the temple of Artemis at Ephesus, the statue of Zeus at Olympia, the Mausoleum at Halicarnassus, the Colossus of Rhodes and the Pharos (lighthouse) at Alexandria

triremes Greek warships powered by oars set in three tiers

Further resources

Books

Amos, H. D. and Lang A. G. P., **These were the Greeks** (Duckworth, 1996)

Camp, John and Fisher, Elizabeth, **Exploring the World of the Ancient Greeks** (Thames & Hudson, 2002)

Chapman, Gillian, **Art from the Past: The Greeks** (Heinemann, 1999)

Dillon, Matthew (editor), **The Ancient Greeks in Their Own Words** (Sutton, 2002)

Macdonald, Fiona, **Strange Histories: The Ancient Greeks** (Belitha, 2003)

Miles, Lesley, **Encyclopedia of Ancient Greece** (Internet-backed), (Usborne, 2003)

Sheehan, Sean, **The British Museum Illustrated Encyclopedia of Ancient Greece**, (British Museum, 2001)

Woodford, Susan, **Introduction to Greek Art** (Duckworth, 1986)

Websites to visit

www.ancientgreece.com
Information on all aspects of ancient Greek life.

www.harpy.uccs.edu/greek/greek.html
Photos of ancient Greek architecture and art.

www.perspicacity.com/elactheatre/library/pedia/greek.htm
A guide to Greek theatre, with information on the origins of Greek drama and famous dramatists.

en.wikipedia.org/wiki/Ancient_philosophy
An introduction to ancient Greek philosophy and philosophers.

www.desy.de/gna/interpedia/greek_myth/story.html
Retells a few stories from Greek myths.

Index